Fifty Scattered Pieces

Gina Marecki

Green Heart Living Press

Fifty Scattered Pieces

ISBN Paperback: 978-1-954493-10-0
ISBN Ebook: 978-1-954493-11-7

Cover artwork: Kendra Tidrick, IG account @k.t.tidrick

Table of Contents

Foreword	7
Introduction	9
Dedication	11
Door	13
The Ditch	14
Sad Soup	15
The Unknown Gulf	16
The Death of the Life	17
Wednesdays	18
Push Me, Pull Me	19
Weights on my Shoulders	20
Abusers Abuse	21
Free	22
The Call	23
Sea of Blue	24
Goodnight Room	25
My To-Do List	26
Drifting Smoke	28
The Dream	29
Wanting...Waiting	30
The Drowning Sea	31
The Unfinished Painting	32
Icy Blue Heat	33

The Edge 34
Wade Through the Swamp 35
Hopes & Dreams 36
The Real Story 37
Don't Cry for Me 38
Mirror, Mirror 40
Feelings 41
Blind 42
Sleep 43
Words 44
Write for Life 45
The Sun 46
When 47
Writer's Block 48
Pieces of Me 49
Heat 51
One Thread 52
The Unravelling 54
The One Thing 55
Prisms of Hope 57
Entangled 59
The Kiss 60
The Longer the Fall 61
Holding On 62
Goodbye 63

Layers 64
The Shift 65
FLY 66
The Magnificent Lie 68
The Truth 69
Space to Feel 71

Foreword

As a publisher, life coach, and social worker, I know the healing power of writing. I've seen countless people pour their hearts out on a page and their lives completely transform as a result.

As a human being who has experienced anxiety, obsessive compulsive disorder, trauma, and depression, healing has gotten me through extremely dark times. I have journals lining the walls of my office from when I was a little kid, through high school, my college years, my life as a young mother, through my divorce, heartbreaks, traumas, and now. The pages are filled with celebration and joys, as well as some things I'd never want anyone to see.

If I did not have writing as a release, the words and fear would have eaten me up inside. There are things that I figured out through writing. There are things I figured out through reading.

Sometimes, when I read the words from my past, I want to say, 'Wake up, kid! Get out!' Sometimes, I laugh and smile at my wild ways. But mostly, I want to reach back and give myself a hug. I want to say, 'Honey, you'll get through this. Don't check out just yet. It gets wayyyyy better. I promise.'

What I love about Gina Marecki's book, "Fifty Scattered Pieces," is that it demonstrates 1) the incredible power of writing to heal and transform, and that 2) healing and growth are possible, no matter what state of misery you find yourself in now.

I can relate to many of Gina' s words because I, too, have felt the darkness wash over me, and not seen any way out. I know what it's like to be there. At that time, reading poems and books that I could relate to fed my soul and gave me nourishment like nothing else would do. Reading sunshine and rainbows at that time just wouldn't cut it.

To meet Gina now is to see someone who helps others grow and transform every day. Through her work, she helps people find their own inner strength and power, just as she once had to find for herself. This book helps us catch a glimpse of the journey it took to get to a place where she could be helping others. It is a message to anyone going through a dark time. It is a message that they are not alone. Others have gone through it. Others have grown through it and now help others. And they can make it through, too. They don't need to go it alone, either. We get it. We understand. And people like us are here to help.

Elizabeth B. Hill, MSW, ACC

Introduction

Have you ever felt beaten and betrayed by the world you lovingly embraced? Have you been faced with an adverse experience that knocked you down and stole your happiness?

I, too, have had that happen...many times. I was a victim of childhood sexual abuse at a young age. Never telling anyone of what I endured, I tried to live a "normal" life. Through my teen years, I followed a path of self-destruction, trying to find something to make me feel normal to no avail. I numbly went through life, graduated high school, earned a degree in college and began a career. Still having low self esteem and hints of my past trauma lurking in the back of my mind, I then found myself in an abusive relationship in early adulthood.

After that traumatic experience, I began to turn my life around, finding God's love, then the love and caring soul of my now husband. We began a life together, creating a wonderful family. Years later, my childhood trauma came hurtling back at me. Anger and rage took over. Depression, anxiety, and panic attacks ensued. My mind and body were haunted by flashbacks and chronic pain. I sought therapy to heal.

During my recovery from depression and anxiety, I found two things that helped me: exercising and writing. I began to make exercise a priority and then I started to write. I created fictional stories based on my feelings; elation from working out, fears from my past, hoping to one day share with the world. I journaled and created poetry and prose of the feelings I held captive.

Now seemed to be an opportune time to share these writings with you. These fifty scattered pieces are pieces of me accumulated over the last several years during my healing.

I share these pieces with you, in hope that you may find comfort with your own scattered, shattered world. Maybe you, too, will pour your feelings onto the page. Maybe you can come to peace with an injustice that was done to you. Maybe you can free yourself of the darkness that has been holding you back from being beautifully, wonderfully you.

Gina

Dedication

Dedicated to those who shine light in the darkness.

Door

The door is wide open
Wide open for me
Which way will I turn?
They say opportunity knocks
But I fear this door may hold
the point of no return.

What if this door holds something evil, something dark?
Maybe it's my opportunity to shine through some light?
Leading the way towards something right.

I hear the knock, but will I answer today?
Maybe this isn't the time to walk away.
I have passed through many a door,
never realizing the strength they held.
I ignored the sound, the light, the calling,
their spell.

There is a door waiting for all of us.
What way will we choose?

The Ditch

Drowning and twisting in the ice cold black
I strain and pull, trying to make it back
To the light and the glow of your love
I see God's sky and draw hope from above
My silent screams are a deafening pitch
The darkness holds lies and tries to bewitch
With temptation and deception
Forever trying to drag me back to that ditch.

Sad Soup

Will you join me for lunch?
As I sit in my hell.

Will you join me my dear?
Even though I don't fare well.

Leave behind the boisterous crowd
The lights so bright
Their laughter so loud.

Welcome to the show, my dear
The chaos I dwell in
Is all that you fear.

You smile as I sit lifeless as the world spins around
The gloomy skies follow me
Dark clouds abound.

Come join me my dear as I sink to the depth
Come sit with me as I fight unseen demons
My dark secret kept.

The sad soup it calls me to drown in the black
It's poisonous brew masked with promises
But once you join me, there is no turning back.

The Unknown Gulf, 3/23/20

COVID-19

The unknown gulf lies before me
No clear picture of a way out for me
Gray and foggy, with murky lines
Tar and mud that threatens to bind
Feeling unsettled, ratcheted up and scared,
I stand before it's hollow mouth my soul bared
I need to step in because it's the only way through
There awaits a promise beyond the bleak, a sky of blue
My heart bleeds out the thickest crimson stream
Tears flood my eyes, not knowing what this all means
I let my prisms of hope fly into the claws of this beast
Unknown if those colors would soon cease
Dropping to my knees, I would have sold my soul
Giving anything to fill this hole.
My faith gives me strength to forge through,
led by a glow of brilliance
I believe we will all make it through this gulf
with utmost resilience.

The Death of the Life

The death of the life I used to live
Gone from my memory, taken from this world
The death of the life I used to live
There is nothing left for me to hold.
Bleak and black, no light shines through
Gasping, grasping, fighting for truth.

The death of the life, that life just moments ago
Torn from my hands and laid to waste.
My treasure, my hope, my heart slammed to the floor
Not cared for by those who abuse with haste.

Blurred lines of the life I once lived
The goodness, the happy times, the love and the friends
All seem murky from the dirt forced into my face
Hate, anger, rage. I am lost in this space.

Help me find that life I once lived
Not the tarnished, burnt and bruised one that smothers me
Help me ashore, breathe of life anew
Let death escape me as God's love shines through.

Wednesdays

Wednesday writings
Wednesday muse
Flowing free from my mind
When you light the fuse
But these words can't describe
How I feel
When you are near.
Small words feel insignificant to the feelings that overwhelm.
How to deal
With what I feel
You can never know
And I will never show...
But if you are reading this, then you may guess this is about you,
And yes, you will get I have always felt this way,
Ever since we first met.

Push Me, Pull Me

Reign me in
Pull me close
I need to have you near

Loosen your hold
Throw me back
Push me far away

You want me
You hate me
Nothing in between

Weights On My Shoulders

My anti-depressant, my anxiety relief,
My pick me up, lift me up, make me so high drug of choice
The rush, the high, the calm, the cool
That heavy load lifts me out of my drowning pool.
Pulse quickens, hard to breathe
Sweat streaming down my face
Straining every muscle to go farther
Heart beating fast, muscles screaming
Hold on, just do it, fight through it, don't think, push harder
Bring it. You got this. Do not break.
The highest of highs beats out any of my lowest of lows
The rush stays with me, long after the weights
are returned to their place
This is the rush that lifts the weight off my shoulders.

Abusers Abuse 6/5/20

The sadness rips through my soul,
I feel the grief
Like a two-ton weight on my back
I cannot breathe.

Black as night, beauty and bright
Drifts to the blue heavens through rays of light
Calling us here to fight the fight.
We hold the torch, we march the march
We scream and cry, heartbroken and scared
Wishing we could have prevented this unthinkable plight

Abusers abuse, these kings given too much power
Breaking the oath of serving for good to serving for evil.
They take, burn, beat, steal, violate, mar, humiliate and kill
Trying to crush the spirits of us all

The abusers abuse.
Let us rise as one, there is no time to lose.

This is all I can offer, this prose from my heart
The knife digs in deep and spills forth this form of art.
I see you and hear you, I feel your pain
I can't know your struggles,
but maybe ones I've endured feel the same

Those abusers abuse
They take, burn, beat and steal
We will rise against them
Our brightness and love to be revealed.
#BLM
#Abusenomore
#Survivors
#Riseupforchildren

Free

Burning
Gripping
Tearing
Ripping
Ridding myself of the pain inside
Cumulative hate, stored in a vault
Set the fire
Feel the flame
Burning it down to piles of ash
The shackles no longer cut my skin
Freeing the grip it once had on me

Blinding
Shining
Glowing
Soaring
Out of the depth and dark murky waters
Rising above like a phoenix
Finally set free.

The Call

Love alight
Shines so bright
How will I make it another night?

The heat rising
The sun blinding
Each day seems to last a lifetime

Waiting for your touch
Feeling it etched on my skin
Another week passes like a year at a time

The day will come
The night will fall
As I wait endlessly for you to call.

Sea of Blue

Sea of Blue draws me in
I stay afloat while I can
Until I sink down again.

You ebb & flow with each breath I take
Bringing the wave that lifts me higher
Lighter than I ever felt before
Hold me there forever more.

The warmth of the sun holds me close
No movement or sound but the beating of my heart.

I do not want to look down so soon
But the wave drops to shore again, alas
Till the sea of blue draws me in again.

Goodnight Room

Tired seeps into my bones
Need for sleep
Rest it evades me
Somewhere out of reach.
Heavy eyes arrive too soon
Black as night
Sleep till noon.

My To-Do List:

Write
Create
Believe
Imagine
Make a new story
Build a character
Make new relationships
Travel new worlds
Try new things
Make your heart race
Find calm
Travel a new road
Visit a faraway place
Find my center
Reach for a new height
Love the Moon
Admire the Sun
Count the stars
And my blessings
Run a race
Pick a fight
Dance to a new song
Sing loudly
Smile broadly
Listen and hear
Play a lot

Laugh from my heart
Cry from my soul
Wonder inside
Ask questions out loud
Try harder
Go slower
Take a different turn
Step up to the plate
Step back for someone else
Learn something new
Try something hard
Share this list

Drifting Smoke

How clear the vision, how close to touch?
For a fleeting moment, I feel the rush.
Then it was gone, like drifting smoke.
Bringing me back, from the dream I woke.

The Dream

Did you ever have that feeling when you woke from a dream
that it could have been true?

It felt so real that you almost couldn't believe it was a dream?

Everything so real you could feel it, taste it,
see everything with such clarity.

It was so utterly amazing
so much better than what was happening in your real life
you would do anything to return to it?

Give up anything,
even your own life
just to feel that way
for one more moment in time.

Wanting...Waiting

Wanting...the more I want the further I slide
Waiting longer, wanting more.
Wanting...but did I genuinely want what I saw?
My eyes were open to the truth
not wanting what was before me
Until it was taken away.
Then I was left
Wanting...
Waiting...

The uneasy feelings come on fast, without warning
and for no apparent reason, but there was a reason.
It hovered below the surface, threatening to flood over
and pull me under
Taking over, making me question everything...

But there was no answer.
No life preserver thrown my way.
Then I'm left
Wanting...
Waiting...

For someone to answer my silent cries for help
Waiting for someone to see...
But also wanting to drown in the deep dark sea.

The Drowning Sea

Drowning in the sea of sorrow that engulfs me.
My arms fight to stay afloat, muscles burn with the effort
Still I sink and swallow the darkness that surrounds me.

Bobbing through waves then through the calm waters
Grasping at energy and life when I can,
a small life preserver that keeps me afloat
Until the next wave of black rises.

Tumbling, turning, caught in the tide,
there is nothing left to do but let it ride.

Calm shores, rays of light come into view
Safety is in sight, but still miles away.

You are the only reason that I hang on and do not let go.
I can breathe knowing I will be on that warm side
of the island with you soon.

You are my only light and my hope in this drowning sea.

The Unfinished Painting

Wanting to paint the picture,
but not knowing where to begin.
The colors overlap and images swim.

Go to the beginning, frame by frame, remembering blues,
oranges, colors of fire and ice.
Red hot flames against cool ice blue skies.

Where to begin?
How to start?
Sketch a line, draw my life.
Pouring out my heart.

Yet there is nothing that lands on the page.

Frozen in time,
never wanting to leave
the images behind my eyes.

Icy Blue Heat

Icy Blue
Cuts my skin straight through
I stack the layers I've built to keep away from you.

Icy Blue
Stabbing heat
Rips through the fabric of my soul
But I still always run back to you.

Icy Blue Heat
Feel the warmth on my skin, summer, sun, ocean waves
Smooth as granite, soft as molded clay
I feel the heat of your glowing rays.

Icy Blue Heat
Fill me with desire
Again, I melt into your raging fire.

The Edge

Far, far, I take it too far.
It's zero to one hundred in my speeding car.
It's never a joy ride,
It's always a race.
Give me the muscle, keep up that pace.

Bumps and roadblocks take up space
Hairpin turns, another police chase.
Flying by, never touching the brakes.
Push it, the rush, do not hesitate.

Far, far, I've gone too far.
Speeding past a shooting star.
But there's no turning back.
I can't live without the chase.

Wade Through the Swamp

I've spent too much time in the murky waters
Much too much time in the grime
I've gotten used to this state of mind
Being alone and down all the time.

Although the sun shines and the river runs quick
This quicksand I'm in is stuck in time
A replay of endless images in my mind.

Stuck in the mud, slow motion grind
Life comes to a halt though the movie continues on rewind.

Haunting darkness closing in.
I'm gasping for breath in this unseen world.

No one sees the hell I'm in.
They only see the mirage I've designed.

The facade, the show, the mask for all to see
But I wonder. I always wonder...
Would they stay if they saw inside the real me?

Hopes & Dreams

My hope, my dreams
My wish is for you to see

To share, to tell
Finally set it all free

It was locked up
Tucked away deep
Then slowly, pieces began to seep

Rising to the surface
The lava overflows
Setting fire to the world I know.
Cleanse and rebirth come after the blaze
The past behind me left in the haze.

Freedom rings from heavens above,
Filled now with unending love.

My hopes, my dreams, my wish I now see
It all lies within reach
Because I am set free.

The Real Story

Should I tell my story?
Should I let it flow?
From the very beginning?
Dare I tell it all?

Should I share my truth?
That one black speck that dropped and spattered
Running and staining my work of art?

Should I set it free?
That one dark tale
That set the wheels in motion
For the script of my life.

To tell, to share, to set it free
There is a price to pay once it's there for all to see.

Will they judge?
Will they run?
Or will they sigh...
And say that same thing happened to me?

When it's time to set it free,
It won't be for them.

I'll do it just for me.

Don't Cry For Me

Don't want your sympathy
Don't want your tears
Don't want your judgement
Or those sideways leers.

Don't want to be known
As the broken one
I am a survivor
A thriver
A warrior
The Resilient One.

One stole control
Another attempted to beat me down
The darkness of my depression tried to overtake me.
But none of those would ever win
Because each time I rose again.

Can't keep me down
Can't silence my voice
I'm here to stay
It's my life, it's my choice.
Don't want your sympathy
Don't want your tears
I understand your desire to try to change what you fear.

But understand the purpose of telling my story
Wasn't told to help you see.

My story was told to set my soul free.

Mirror, Mirror

Cracked mirror mirror on the wall
How can I see myself at all?
The lines cut deep across my face, etching every flaw
The slash under my eye, dark and jagged
Are these lines for real or are they from the broken remains
from my mirror?

Shattered mirror mirror on the wall
Will I ever be the same at all?
The missing pieces leave a void making me wonder,
Was I ever really whole at all?
The shards catch the morning light,
reflecting the beauty amid the cracks.
The black of evening casts the shadows of demons
and darkness across my face
Making me want to flee this space

Demolished mirror mirror from the wall
Smashed to pieces on the floor
Anger and rage taking flight, terminating this mask of fright.
I finally flee this cave of blackness bleak
Finding the sun, warmed by its heat.
Drawn to the sea which reflects my image back to me.
Whole, glowing, one, finally free.

Feelings

Scattered
Shattered
Screaming light

Clawing
Gnawing
Feeling fright

Desperate
Isolate
Black as night

Blind

Eyes burning fighting to stay awake
The light too bright
The noise too loud
Overstimulated can't take the crowd
Shut it out
Shut it down
Block it out
Ignore the sound

Bring me to the black
The darkness of night
Numb to sounds
Numb to sight

Relief comes when the pain is gone
The feeling of nothing weighing me down.

Sleep

The countdown begins
The numbers spiral by
Curving and turning down the never ending stairwell.
I count and I count my way out of this hell.

The darkness wraps around me
but I see all
every world, every memory
the deeper I fall

Rock in the boat
The hammock encases me
Watching the sheep
as they fly high above me

Sleep it evades me
I dream of that moment far away
when my eyes grow heavy,
slipping into that imagined world
as my own world fades to grey.

Words

Words swirl and tumble through my brain
Cascading from my hands onto the page
Speaking of truths, of nightmares and dreams
The ones that make you sigh
The ones that make you scream.

Words trail across the screen
A life longed to be lived or a horror unseen.
My fingers spin tales with the greatest of ease
Yet at times completing a thought
I do not have the keys.

Write for Life

Write and write all through the night
I try to find the words but nothing comes to mind

I search and seek the words to write
But none I find

The lover's kiss, the fighter's fist,
I just can't get the gist

Write and write through the night I pray
So many words, yet I find nothing to say

Will anyone listen?
Will anyone care?

I see my words drift into the air.

The Sun

My sun, my sun
My only one
Bright as a fire
Roaring to life

My moon, my moon
For you I swoon
White as the snow
Lighting my way

My star, my star
I know where you are
You lead me along
Guiding me home

My sky, my sky
To you I fly
You hold the sun, moon and stars
Endless heavens and glories above.

When

When will it end, this vision I seek?
When will it end, my feeling so weak?

When will it be time for calm waters and shade?
When will it be time for freedom to cascade?

When will it begin, that love everlasting?
When will it begin, without shadows overcasting?

When will it be, this ebb and this flow?
When will it be? I may never know.

Writer's Block

Writing prompt 1
Think of the sun
I thought of the sun and my words became black.

Writing prompt 2
Think of the dew
I tried to think of the dew and all I could conjure
was a raging flood.

Writing prompt 3
Think of a majestic tree
I imagined tall trees and all I remembered
was running through the haunted wood.

Writing prompt 4
Think of amore
I thought of deep love and no words filled my page.

Pieces of Me

Pieces of me chiseled away
Those pieces of me scattered like dust in the wind
Floating, fading
Until their shine was dimmed

Left with porous holes that absorb the blackness,
dark as night
Pieces of me that were taken out of sight
Those pieces stripped without a trace
Leaving me spiraling to an unknown space

The empty, numb feeling of the gaping wounds
hiding beneath the surface
Those once bright spots, tarnished and burnished
Soon filled with sadness, anger, hate and rage
Feelings I wished to assuage
Armed and determined to find what was taken from me
Drawing from a newfound strength
Searching, seeking
Fighting a battle, going to any length

The harder I fought, the less ground I gained
Weakened and scarred, my question remained
Those pieces of me, where did they fly?
I sought to find answers as I reached to God's sky

Finding refuge and healing by the sea
Calm breath, warm light, sea of blue, golden ray
Opening my eyes to the new day

Slowly with the incoming tide, those pieces floated ashore
Washing away the hate until it shows no more.

Love filled the empty caverns with light
Prisms of colors taking flight
as the darkness was unleashed into the sea
Completing the work of art I was meant to be

Heat

The numbness is a void that needs to be filled
Bring the force, bring the heat
Put the intensity on repeat.

I feel so much yet nothing at all
I climb then stumble and ultimately fall.

I need the intensity, I need the heat
But scared to be burned
Scared of defeat

Searching for that rush, searching for that heat
I cover miles yet no progress made
What will it take to make me complete?

One Thread

Hanging on, hanging on by that thread
The thread I want to pull
The one that keeps it all together
Can't I just pull and free myself of the snarl?
How can this one thread hold so much?

The small bump in the rug,
The pull in my sweater
Smooth it away, bury it deep
Don't look now, it's beginning to seep
The string leads me to another layer,
the one that binds
The vine that clings and climbs

Hang on, hang on tight
Don't tug hard, that one just might
Be the one to tear a hole
A deep chasm burrowed down into the dark
The place where evil things lurk

Stay, stay in the light
Hang on, hold on tight
That last thread thin and bare
Exposing me, leaving me where I need to take care

Stay strong, hang on
Keep it together
Sew those seams
Fix those tears
Keep the faith
Say prayers

Hang on, hang on to that thread
The thread of my life
It's all I hold onto to keep it together.

The Unravelling

Beautiful fabric
Stitched with care
Rich in beauty
Warmth fills the seams

The stitching is flawless
at first glance
The closer you look
you'll find the loose end

That one small thread
not sewn into place
That one small loose end
will be its undoing

A pull through the center
tangled in knots
The unravelling begins
undoing the pattern

Those loose ends always tend to unravel.

The One Thing

The one thing you should know
is that I don't like the dark
The infinite black surrounds me
the walls around me stark.

The next thing you should know
is I have this recurring dream
It's full of chaos and dread,
I usually wake with a scream.

The third thing you should know
is there is a hole deep inside me.
A void that cannot be fulfilled
though I attempt at it constantly.

Another thing you should know
is I'm quick with a temper.
Not giving in
I will never surrender.

The next thing you should know
I'm loyal to a fault.
I will fight to keep you,
your trust in a vault.

The last thing you should know
is I'm a mystery

You will never truly know
a single thing about me.

Prisms of Hope

The deep hue of purple, brands the logo of my business, adorns t-shirts, business cards, the sign on my door and all things GFitness. Shades of burgundy, plum and wine, my uniform representing strength and balance, my hashtags with hearts follow every post #areyouready? #stronger and #resilience.

This magical mysterious hue reminds me of time long before, of my daughters and a time when they were small. Laughter, kisses and curly hair, purple, lavender, pink ribbons, bows and headbands everywhere, littered the bathroom counter, filled baskets and drawers. My Little Ponies, Disney Princesses and play dough, then my son came along adding the shades of midnight, cobalt and all shades of blue, matchbox cars and legos.

But not known to most, below these bright prisms of colors I drowned in the blackest of depression and gnawing anxiety, nightmares and flashbacks that I couldn't escape, threatening to cover my colorful world and blind me. The depression black as tar and anxiety, red as molten lava threatened to pull me under and trap me below its hardened surface. Plagued with memories of things that happened a lifetime ago, suppressed and pushed down, had nowhere to go. The tidal wave broke through the faulty foundation I built as cover. Feelings of sadness and rage increased in severity, no longer able to hover.

I fought to stay with my colorful prisms as the inky waters flooded over.

Light lavender and blue giggles, purple lollipops, pink glitter, sparkles and blue boy blocks and bright yellow trucks sent rays of hope my way. My oldest daughter's memory of growing up in a "purple house," which consisted of her bedroom of pale lilac and apparently her view of the world. My second daughter's deep violet bedroom and her way of pronouncing purple without the "r." My son's addition of blues, greens and golds; sports galore became my focus, all an attempt to keep me from feeling hopeless.

My daily fight to be strong with silent screams to right this wrong. The fear and sadness of not being a good mother clawed at my soul. When my patience wore thin and I would yell or shut down, I prayed those lilac, lavender, blue memories filled my children's hearts and were the ones that won out.

Now as adults, my children send me purple heart emojis and give me gifts of that color. Purple by definition invokes spirituality, creativity, calm, helping those in need and a draw to educate the masses, meditation, inspiration, compassion, ambition, and strong intuition.

Purple is made up of the calm stability of blue mixed with the fierce energy of red. Maybe the purple I hold so dearly reminds me of what I'd overcome. Maybe I'd unknowingly harnessed the essence of this color. Subconsciously aware that beyond the black tar which threatened to pull me under, the only thing that kept me afloat were my vivid prisms of color.

Entangled

The challenge, the wonder, the question.
Never an answer
Drawing in and getting stronger.
Ready to run, ready to soar.
Needing the heat, wanting it more.

Your invisible web draws me in
Then it is too late
You have me trapped, ensnared.
But would I flee
If you set me free?

The Kiss

If I could wish this kiss
I would wish this kiss to exist
If I could wish this kiss
I would wish this kiss morning and night.
If I could wish this kiss
I would wish it to be a tattoo on my skin.
If I could wish this kiss
I would wish this kiss to never exist,
To forever be erased from my memory
That way I would never have to wish for this kiss to exist.

The Longer the Fall

Feelings so strong
So intense
Blinding, burning,
Twisting, turning,
Draining me of energy
Needing to stay strong
Keep fighting
Intensity builds once again
Climbing
The higher the risk
The longer the fall
Hold on tight
Once more
So intense
Blinding, burning
Twisting, turning
Give me the courage before I fall.

Holding On

Don't let go
I need to fly, to soar above the clouds
I need it a little more but
Not able to keep up
Or maintain the height
But trying each day
Through every fight
Keep me close
Forever near
Keep me strong
Help me lose my fear

Goodbye

It will be sad to say goodbye
It will be sad when the curtain closes

I know it's time, but I've avoided
That inevitable drop of the axe

I held onto promises made
While you spun those tales of woe

Hanging on I would never let go
Leading me along, always in the know

That day would come
You'd be gone

But now I'm strong
I can stand alone
It's no longer about you
Or being tied to that stage.
It's about me
And being

Free.

Layers

Peel back the layers
One by one
Hurts at first
Then you become numb.

Blinding pain that first layer torn
Exposed to the world sheared and shorn.

After time, the air heals
Making the outer shell strong

The daggers you throw can no longer puncture
I stand protected by this impenetrable structure.

The Shift

Back in the day
One time I could
Remember when I did
I used to be
I never was
I wished I did
I wish I was
I regret not
I always wanted
But there was that one time...
I won
I beat
I was strong, skinny, pretty
I dominated
I passed
I achieved
I loved
I cared
I cured
I held
I was a friend...
I hold no regrets.

FLY

Beautiful bird
Trapped in a cage
Your song echoes across the stage.

Beautiful bird
You fly about spreading your wings
Pushing the limits, you continue to sing.

Beautiful bird
Your colors majestic
Bold and deep, your aura angelic.

As time goes on, your song ceases
No one there to hear those beautiful pieces.

Your flight diminishes with caged in walls
Your flight to the heavens now stalled.

Your colors diminished
Beaten, held down, no light, tattered and blemished.

Keep singing you beautiful bird
Don't let them end this
Regain your strength
Resist the abyss.

Take flight push your limits
Don't let that prison hold you in
Find that flight
Use your strength from within.

Push through the fire
Trudge through the muck
Your colors will shine
In this trap, no longer be stuck.

Fly my bird
You hold the key
It all comes from you
The power to be set free.

The Magnificent Lie

Sigh
I cry
But no one sees
My strength covers up
I'm weak in the knees

Scream
And yell
But no one hears
My silent hell

Fear
Taking over
My confidence masks
The fearful child facing these tasks

Die
I have died
I look alive
But my face covers this magnificent lie.

The Truth

Does it make you uneasy?
These truths that I've told.
Does it make you feel queasy?
Like something rotted with mold.

So sorry for your discomfort, but truth be told
I honestly don't care; I know that sounds cold.

Imagine how I felt having kept these things inside
Tucked down deep, in corners they hide.
Eating away at my body over all this time
Pain, black, evil, covering my insides with slime.

I'm giving it away now, I'm free at last
For that black creature is now an outcast.

I'm strong because of my past
This clearing has healed me.

These are all the scattered pieces of me.

Space to Feel

I'm grateful for the unending love and support from my husband, Vaughan. Thank you for being my biggest fan and my rock. I'm thankful to God, my family and friends. Thank you to Mary Roy for your unwavering belief in my message and for those extra pushes. Thank you to Elizabeth Hill from Green Heart Living for believing in me and in my writing. Thank you to Kendra Tidrick (@k.t.tidrick Instagram) for capturing the essence of this book with her beautiful cover artwork.

Writing opened a door for me enabling me to heal and set free the anger I had trapped inside. Turning fifty last year, I decided it was time to share my journey with others. I collected these scattered pieces from my journals and notebooks with a hope to have at least fifty. During the pandemic, I wrote and ended up surpassing that number.

I hope you will use this space to feel what you are feeling. It may be difficult to begin. Sometimes you just need to write the first word that comes to mind and then an entire world will open before you.

Space to Feel

Space to Feel

Space to Feel

Space to Feel

About Gina Marecki

Gina Marecki grew up in New City, New York. After high school, she attained an associate degree and moved to Boston, Massachusetts to live with her sister. She specialized in marketing and promotional meeting management at John Hancock Mutual Funds for six years. During that time, she completed her bachelor's degree at Boston College. While working at John Hancock, she met her now husband, Vaughan. Gina and Vaughan were married in 1997 and lived in Hingham, Massachusetts for one year before moving to Simsbury, Connecticut to start and raise their family.

At age 38, Gina had been battling depressive and anxiety symptoms for several years. She sought the help of a behavioral therapist and worked to overcome past childhood sexual trauma. She found exercise and writing helped her through dark moments. Adding heavy weightlifting, intense cardio, Z-Health, a neurological based training program and Muay Thai kickboxing to her arsenal, she fought her silent battle.

Gina pursued her passion for fitness by becoming a Certified Personal Trainer and Women's Fitness Specialist in 2012. After four years she expanded her business and opened G Fitness and Wellness studio in Simsbury, Connecticut. Her clients include regular fitness enthusiasts, athletes, those who have suffered past injuries, depression, trauma, autoimmune diseases and cancer. She uses her kickboxing experience to help women feel empowered. Her marketing background has helped her to promote and grow her business.

Gina began creative writing when faced with depression and recently participated in writer's workshops with the goal of publishing a work of fiction. Gina resides in Simsbury with her husband, Vaughan of over 23 years. They have three grown children and two cats.

Also by Gina Marecki

Transformation 2020

Green Heart Living Press Publications

Success in Any Season

Redefining Masculinity

Grow Smarter: Collaboration Secrets to Transform Your Income and Impact

Transformation 2020

Transformation 2020 Companion Journal

The Great Pause: Blessings & Wisdom from COVID-19

The Great Pause Journal

Love Notes: Daily Wisdom for the Soul

Green Your Heart, Green Your World: Avoid Burnout, Save the World and Love Your Life

www.ingramcontent.com/pod-product-compliance
Lightning Source LLC
LaVergne TN
HW021618080426
510LV00019B/2639
9 7 8 1 9 5 4 4 9 3 1 0 0 *